Snares and Swindles in Bridge

The most formidable opponents at this game are the tricky players whose cards cannot always be taken at face value. Their profit accrues not only when they are perpetrating swindles but also when you wrongly suspect that they are.

In this little book the authors show you how to acquire a reputation as a tricky player by expanding your repertoire of deceptive plays. The examples are clear and well-chosen, ranging from spectacular bluffs to subtle false cards aimed at persuading your opponents that black is white.

After absorbing the simple techniques explained in this book, you will be a more complete player, capable of masking your weakness, concealing your strength, and throwing a smoke-screen over your real intentions.

The authors have won equal distinction as players and as writers on the game. For many years Roger Trézel was an automatic choice for the French International Team, as was Terence Reese for the British. Both are European and World Champions.

D0735382

Master Bridge Series
General Editor: Hugh Kelsey

A distinguished new series which contains
books by the world's foremost experts on all
aspects of the game, ranging from Hugh Kelsey's
own book for beginners to books on advanced
techniques of bidding and play.

Terence Reese and Roger Trézel

Snares and Swindles in Bridge

LONDON
VICTOR GOLLANCZ LTD
in association with Peter Crawley

© Terence Reese and Roger Trézel 1977

First published in 1977 by Ward Lock Limited
Second impression April 1979

ISBN 0 575 02633 2

Printed and bound by R. J. Acford Ltd, Chichester, Sussex

Playing card on cover reproduced by
courtesy of Waddingtons Playing Card Co Ltd

Introduction

by Terence Reese

The play of the cards at bridge is a big subject, capable of filling many large books. Some years ago Roger Trézel, the great French player and writer, had the idea of breaking up the game into several books of the present length, each dealing with one of the standard forms of technique. He judged, quite rightly as it turned out, that this scheme would appeal both to comparative beginners, who would be able to learn the game by stages, and to experienced players wishing to extend their knowledge of a particular branch of play.

We have now worked together on an English version, profiting from his experience. The first four titles in the series are:

1 Safety Plays in Bridge
2 Blocking and Unblocking Plays in Bridge
3 Elimination Play in Bridge
4 Snares and Swindles in Bridge

Other titles are in preparation.

Snares and Swindles

Deceptive plays belong to a class of their own, because of the personal and psychological element. A perfect elimination or squeeze play will be as effective against a world champion as against the opponent in your next rubber, but the success of a deceptive play may seem to depend on a variety of circumstances, such as the smoothness with which it is performed and the quality of the player whom you seek to deceive. To some extent that is true, but there is, nevertheless, a technique to be learned. Your opponent, if an experienced player, may *suspect* that you are using one of the standard forms of deception; but he may not be sure, for the essence of a good deceptive play is that the card might be genuine, or it might be a trap. Moreover, as will appear from the examples that follow, there are numerous situations where a particular card *must* be played to give the opponent a guess.

To be adept in this form of play, therefore, it is not necessary to be a master of psychology or to play against 'simple' opponents. Many plays are more effective against a strong opponent than a weak one, who will not even see the trap. If you possess a good repertoire of snares and swindles, they will win you a great number of tricks, and one day you may have the satisfaction of bringing off a deceptive play that is not even 'in the book'.

Part I: Deception in attack

Example 1

Are you ready to plunge in at the deep end? Then here is an attractive play which is quite easy to perform but would scarcely occur to a player who had not seen something like it before.

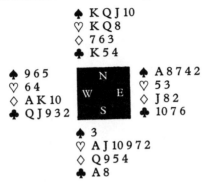

♠ K Q J 10
♡ K Q 8
◇ 7 6 3
♣ K 5 4

♠ 9 6 5
♡ 6 4
◇ A K 10
♣ Q J 9 3 2

N W E S

♠ A 8 7 4 2
♡ 5 3
◇ J 8 2
♣ 10 7 6

♠ 3
♡ A J 10 9 7 2
◇ Q 9 5 4
♣ A 8

After a pass by West, North opens one no trump, and South bids four hearts, the final contract.

West leads the king of diamonds, on which his partner plays the two. West switches to the queen of clubs. Having taken this trick, what can you do to avoid the loss of a spade and two more diamonds?

You can do nothing! You have missed your chance.

As West had passed originally and was already marked with A K of diamonds and, probably, Q J of clubs, you could be sure that East would hold the ace of spades and would fire a diamond through the queen as soon as he gained the lead. It was essential, therefore, to lay a trap for West.

On the queen of clubs you play low from both hands. Unless West is extremely smart (and knows that you are, too), he will continue with another club. Now you win with the ace, draw two rounds of trumps, finishing in dummy, and discard the three of spades on the king of clubs. Then you ruff out the ace of spades, return to dummy with a third round of trumps, and discard your diamond losers on the established spades.

Example 2

The deception illustrated below has been around for many years.
Indeed, you may find something like it in Culbertson's *Contract
Bridge Red Book on Play,* published in the early 1930s. Judging from
the standard of modern defence, it is possible to pick holes in the
play. But that does not affect the value of the example. In less
obvious form the deception is still capable of winning many contracts.

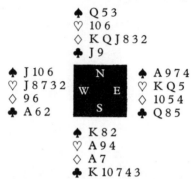

```
                    ♠ Q 5 3
                    ♡ 10 6
                    ◇ K Q J 8 3 2
                    ♣ J 9
    ♠ J 10 6           N           ♠ A 9 7 4
    ♡ J 8 7 3 2    W       E       ♡ K Q 5
    ◇ 9 6                          ◇ 10 5 4
    ♣ A 6 2            S           ♣ Q 8 5
                    ♠ K 8 2
                    ♡ A 9 4
                    ◇ A 7
                    ♣ K 10 7 4 3
```

South opens one club, North responds one diamond, and South bids
one no trump. North would be wise to bid simply two diamonds,
perhaps, but instead he advances to two no trumps, and South goes
to three no trumps.

West leads the three of hearts, and East plays the queen. Technically,
South should hold up the ace until the third round, for if hearts are
5-3 and East holds both black aces, there are genuine chances to make
the contract. However, South may reasonably decide that his best
chance lies in deceptive play. Not wanting to make it obvious to both
defenders that he is wide open in hearts, he captures the first trick,
lays down the ace of diamonds, and then leads the king of spades.

Thinking that declarer is seeking to establish an entry to the table,
East lets the king of spades hold. With eight tricks in the bag, South
next leads the king of clubs. West, falling into the same trap as his
partner, declines to part with the ace lest this establish the jack of
clubs as an entry card for the diamonds. South then runs for home.

As we said, it is easy to criticize the defence. Good players are careful to signal when declarer plays on a long suit held by dummy; thus, West had a chance to show an even number of diamonds by dropping the nine on the first round, and East's play of the four should have indicated an odd number. Furthermore, West should have realized that South could not hold the king of spades, A K of hearts, the ace of diamonds, and K Q of clubs.

Nevertheless, there are many occasions when this type of play by declarer is less easy to read. Note, in particular, the lead of the king of clubs. When dummy has a suit such as J x x x x and declarer holds K x x or K x, it is surprising how often the king will be allowed to hold.

Example 3

Many deceptive plays depend for success on the timing and manner of their execution. Do not misunderstand this remark. We are not suggesting that the critical card should be played with unusual speed or emphasis or any other form of legerdemain: simply that its role should not be apparent.

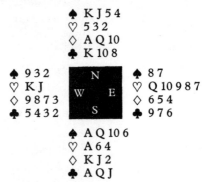

♠ K J 5 4
♡ 5 3 2
♢ A Q 10
♣ K 10 8

♠ 9 3 2   ♠ 8 7
♡ K J   ♡ Q 10 9 8 7
♢ 9 8 7 3   ♢ 6 5 4
♣ 5 4 3 2   ♣ 9 7 6

♠ A Q 10 6
♡ A 6 4
♢ K J 2
♣ A Q J

South plays in six spades, and West leads the nine of diamonds.

Even if you have not studied our little book on elimination play, you will probably realize that declarer's only chance to avoid the loss of two heart tricks is to create a situation in which a defender is forced to allow a ruff-and-discard. In short, South must aim at this end position:

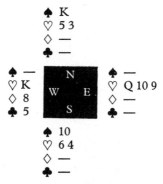

The next round of hearts is won by West, who is obliged to lead one of the minor suits, permitting South to dispose of his second loser in hearts.

But this plan has an obvious weakness: if declarer draws trumps, cashes the winning diamonds and clubs, then lays down the ace of hearts, West, if not completely asleep, will drop his king of hearts under the ace.

To make this defence as difficult as possible South should play a heart to the ace at trick two. A first-class player in West's position might still drop the king—but at least you will have made it more difficult for him.

This type of play is made with many, less obvious combinations. For example, a side suit is divided in this way:

$$
\begin{array}{c}
\text{J 7 6 4 3} \\
\text{Q 5} \qquad\qquad \text{K 10 9} \\
\text{A 8 2}
\end{array}
$$

If South plays off the ace towards the end of the play, having eliminated the other suits, West may realize that to win two tricks in the suit he must unblock the queen; but if declarer lays down the ace at an early stage, the defence is not easy to find.

Example 4

The object of many deceptive plays is to present the defender with a guess that may be difficult to resolve. This situation often occurs at trick one in a suit contract:

```
            A Q 7 5 3 2
    10                    K 8 6 4
            J 9
```

West leads the ten of a side suit that has been bid by the dummy. From South's angle it is likely that the lead is a singleton and almost certain that the finesse will lose. The best plan may be to go up with the ace, dropping the jack from hand, draw trumps, then lead low from the table. This may present East with an awkward decision: to go up with the king might be fatal if South held the singleton.

Here, the same stratagem is used because East is marked on the bidding with the critical king.

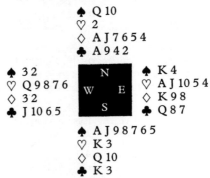

```
                    ♠ Q 10
                    ♡ 2
                    ◇ A J 7 6 5 4
                    ♣ A 9 4 2
    ♠ 3 2                           ♠ K 4
    ♡ Q 9 8 7 6      N              ♡ A J 10 5 4
    ◇ 3 2         W     E           ◇ K 9 8
    ♣ J 10 6 5       S              ♣ Q 8 7
                    ♠ A J 9 8 7 6 5
                    ♡ K 3
                    ◇ Q 10
                    ♣ K 3
```

East is the dealer at love all, and the bidding goes:

SOUTH	WEST	NORTH	EAST
—	—	—	1 ♡
dble	3 ♡	4 ◇	pass
4 ♠	pass	5 ♠	pass
6 ♠	pass	pass	pass

After this ambitious display, South should not be surprised to find that his contract depends on two finesses, one of which is likely to be right, the other wrong.

West leads the seven of hearts, the ace wins, and the jack is returned. South's best plan is to lead the queen of diamonds to the ace and play the queen of spades from dummy. East covers, a spade is led to the ten, and a low diamond is led from the table.

What will East do now? From his point of view, if South held a singleton diamond and K x x of clubs, to put in the king would be fatal; he might, therefore, play low on the second diamond, allowing South's ten to win the trick.

It is true that this trap would not work against expert defenders. West, on the first round of diamonds, would play the three, preparing to play high-low with an even number. This would be enough to tell East that South's queen was not a singleton, for with 10 3 2 West would play the two on the first round, not the three. Thus, there is a lesson for the defence here, as well as for the attack.

Example 5

Sometimes it will be very plain to the declarer, after the opening lead, that an immediate ruff is threatened. On such occasions it may be possible, by means of a spectacular false card, to deflect the opponents from the obvious defence.

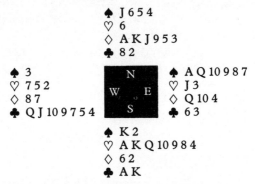

```
                    ♠ J 6 5 4
                    ♡ 6
                    ◇ A K J 9 5 3
                    ♣ 8 2
  ♠ 3                 N              ♠ A Q 10 9 8 7
  ♡ 7 5 2        W         E         ♡ J 3
  ◇ 8 7                               ◇ Q 10 4
  ♣ Q J 10 9 7 5 4    S              ♣ 6 3
                    ♠ K 2
                    ♡ A K Q 10 9 8 4
                    ◇ 6 2
                    ♣ A K
```

North-South are vulnerable, and West, the dealer, begins with a pre-emptive three clubs. The bidding continues:

SOUTH	WEST	NORTH	EAST
—	3 ♣	3 ◇	3 ♠
4 NT	pass	5 ◇	pass
6 ♡	pass	pass	pass

West leads the three of spades, and South realizes, with a swift pang of regret, that it would have been more intelligent to bid the slam in no trumps. However, all is not lost. When East plays the ace of spades, South releases the king!

Even if East is familiar with this particular deception, the odds are that he will switch to a club rather than risk establishing dummy's jack of spades. South wins with the ace, and as there is no hurry to take the diamond finesse he runs down the trumps, arriving at this position:

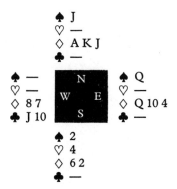

On the last heart the jack of spades is thrown from dummy, and East is squeezed.

This kind of trap can also be laid when the critical suit is 'the other way up':

$$J 9 6 3$$
$$A Q 10 8 4 \qquad 2$$
$$K 7 5$$

West, who has overcalled in this suit, leads the ace. If South plays low, West will have no reason not to play another round, which his partner will ruff. South (who has another long suit in dummy on which he can later take discards) drops the king under the ace, and West may now turn his attention elsewhere.

Example 6

Much of the art of deception consists not in brilliant tactical strokes but in the subtle choice of card—perhaps just a six instead of a four. The idea, usually, is to create in the mind of a defender the impression that his partner has played an encouraging card. When the declarer wants a suit to be continued, it is generally good policy to emit 'signals' just as though he were the partner of the opening leader.

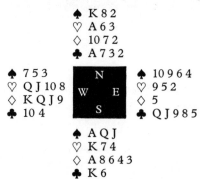

Playing a strong no trump, South conceals his diamond suit and opens one no trump. North raises to three no trumps, and West leads the king of diamonds.

South has eight tricks on top and the only chance for a ninth lies in establishing the fifth diamond. However, if he captures the king with the ace and returns a diamond, West will surely turn to hearts, and the defence will make three diamonds and two hearts before South can arrive at the fifth diamond.

Declarer's best plan, therefore, is to gain a 'tempo' by ducking the first lead and encouraging West to play a second round. This will put South ahead in the race. It is good play, moreover, when East drops the five of diamonds to play the six from hand. West, missing the four and three, may well conclude that his partner has played an encouraging card.

This type of stratagem can be employed on many occasions when declarer is strong on the suit lead. For example:

A 5

J 9 6 3   10 4

K Q 8 7 2

South is in three no trumps and West leads the three of the suit shown. Dummy plays low, and East contributes the ten. South can be sure that he has a loser in the suit, and it is good play to follow with the seven. The situation may not be clear to East and he will probably return the four to dummy's ace. As before, South gains a tempo, the opponents having obligingly established his best suit.

Example 7

Sometimes more spectacular play may be needed to ensure a favourable continuation. Observe the declarer's tactics on the following deal.

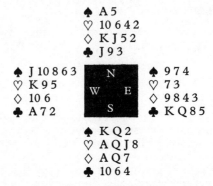

```
                   ♠ A 5
                   ♡ 10 6 4 2
                   ◇ K J 5 2
                   ♣ J 9 3
  ♠ J 10 8 6 3                   ♠ 9 7 4
  ♡ K 9 5          N             ♡ 7 3
  ◇ 10 6       W       E         ◇ 9 8 4 3
  ♣ A 7 2          S             ♣ K Q 8 5
                   ♠ K Q 2
                   ♡ A Q J 8
                   ◇ A Q 7
                   ♣ 10 6 4
```

South is in three no trumps, no suit having been mentioned, and West leads the jack of spades.

Let us suppose, first, that South plays the hand without guile. With eight tricks in sight, he goes up with the ace of spades and runs the ten of hearts to the king.

Now West, who has seen his partner play the four of spades at trick one and South the two, may well conclude that South holds K Q x. As declarer has played on hearts, he probably has tricks there as well. It therefore becomes essential to look for tricks in a minor suit—specifically, in clubs. West will switch to the ace of clubs, hoping that partner has either ace of diamonds and Q 10 x x of clubs, or, less likely, K Q x x of clubs. This second chance turns up, and the contract is defeated.

Now let's go back to the first trick. South should recognize that he does not need more than two spade tricks for game: he can expect to make at least three tricks in hearts and four in diamonds. To avert a switch to clubs he should drop the queen of spades under dummy's ace at trick one. West will assume that declarer has K Q alone, and when he comes in with the king of hearts, he will surely play a second spade.

Example 8

We look next at a number of situations where the declarer has a chance to tempt a defender into covering an honour. To cover an honour with an honour is, of course, very often correct play, but it may also be a calamitous error.

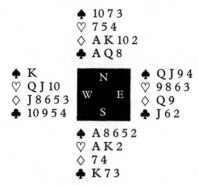

South opens one spade, and North responds two diamonds. Whether South should rebid two spades or two no trumps or even two hearts is a moot point, depending on the system played. In any case, the final contract is four spades, and West leads the queen of hearts.

South captures the first trick, and evidently the contract is going to depend on whether he is destined to lose two trump tricks or three. If trumps are 3-2, any play will serve, while if they are 4-1, it may seem as though three tricks must be lost. And so they will be if declarer makes the lazy play of leading the ace from hand or low towards the ten.

Instead, he should lay a trap into which East may fall if he holds Q J 9 x or K J 9 x. A diamond is led to the king and then the ten of spades is led from the table. If East covers with the jack, then one of his trump tricks goes out of the window.

We hasten to say—in case the point had occurred to you—that the cover is quite wrong on the East hand. The object of covering an honour with an honour is to promote a low card for one defender or the other, and playing the jack on the ten cannot possibly have that effect. Still, the fact remains that half the bridge-playing population would cover—and argue about it afterwards as well!

Example 9

Observe this combination in diamonds and consider how you would play it to lose only one trick, in the absence of any special indication:

J 6 5 3

A 9 7 4 2

If they are 2-2, no problem arises; if 3-1, the best chance is to play off the ace, which gains when East has a singleton king or queen.

But suppose all the indications are that West is likely to be short in the suit; then the jack from dummy is a more promising play.

♠ A K 6 2
♡ 3
◇ J 6 5 3
♣ A Q 9 2

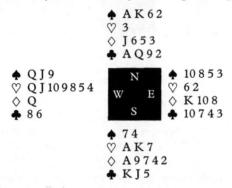

♠ Q J 9   ♠ 10 8 5 3
♡ Q J 10 9 8 5 4 ♡ 6 2
◇ Q   ◇ K 10 8
♣ 8 6   ♣ 10 7 4 3

♠ 7 4
♡ A K 7
◇ A 9 7 4 2
♣ K J 5

West opens three hearts, and North doubles for take-out. The bidding continues:

SOUTH	WEST	NORTH	EAST
—	3 ♡	dble	pass
4 ♡	pass	4 ♠	pass
5 ◇	pass	6 ◇	pass
pass	pass		

West leads the queen of hearts against six diamonds, and South wins with the king. As West is likely to have seven hearts and his partner only two, it is natural to place East with the length in diamonds. Playing off the ace can hardly be right, therefore. Instead, South should cross to dummy with a spade and lead the jack of diamonds from the table. As in the preceding example, it would be poor play for East to cover—but it happens!

Note, also, that when South leads the jack from dummy, he is not just playing for a mistake: he is taking the best legitimate chance (still assuming that West is far more likely than East to hold a singleton). The distribution may be:

$$J653$$
$$10 \qquad KQ8$$
$$A9742$$

Now the lead of the jack wins against any defence.

Example 10

To cause the defenders to crash the king and queen of a suit is a satisfying achievement; to induce a crash of the king and ace is even better.

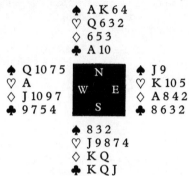

♠ A K 6 4
♥ Q 6 3 2
♦ 6 5 3
♣ A 10

♠ Q 10 7 5   N   ♠ J 9
♥ A   W   E   ♥ K 10 5
♦ J 10 9 7   S   ♦ A 8 4 2
♣ 9 7 5 4   ♣ 8 6 3 2

♠ 8 3 2
♥ J 9 8 7 4
♦ K Q
♣ K Q J

Although there are four top losers in the two hands, it is not so easy for North-South to stay short of four hearts.

West leads the jack of diamonds, East wins with the ace and returns a diamond. It looks as though a spade must be lost and at least two hearts—quite possibly three. However, South crosses to the ace of clubs and leads the queen of hearts from the table.

Once again, it is probably wrong for East to cover, but the situation may not be altogether clear to him. For example, South might hold A J 9 x x, and in that case the best chance for a trump trick is to give him a guess on the second round. As the cards lie, of course, the cover is fatal. West wins with the ace and an angry look. The next trump is led from dummy, and East's 10 x falls to a finesse.

Before we leave this subject, here are two more plays of the same kind:

J 7 6 4

—   Q 10 8

A K 9 5 3 2

South is not intending to take any finesse, but to put East under pressure he begins by leading the jack from dummy. If East is so foolish as to cover with the queen, the lie of the suit is revealed.

9 4 2

Q   J 10 8 3

A K 7 6 5

It looks as though South, playing in no trumps, is bound to lose two tricks against any 4-1 division. However, he begins by leading the nine from dummy. If East covers with the ten, thinking it can make no difference, South wins with the ace, felling the queen, and returns the seven to East's eight; when next in dummy he can pick up the J 3 by a finesse.

Example 11

One of the most important elements in deceptive play is to conceal from the opponents the number of tricks they need to make in a particular suit. Take the common situation where declarer has x x of a suit in hand, K J x in dummy. Before the pattern of the deal has appeared, it is good play to lead towards the K J x. If West has the ace, but not the queen, you put him under some pressure. For all he knows, you might have a singleton and be intending to snatch a vital trick with the king. He may, therefore, be tempted to go up with the ace, solving a guess; and if he plays low without any sign of anxiety, there are grounds for supposing that he may hold the queen, but not the ace.

The following hand is a variation on that theme:

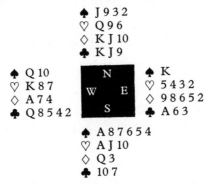

```
              ♠ J 9 3 2
              ♡ Q 9 6
              ◇ K J 10
              ♣ K J 9
  ♠ Q 10          N          ♠ K
  ♡ K 8 7                    ♡ 5 4 3 2
  ◇ A 7 4     W       E      ◇ 9 8 6 5 2
  ♣ Q 8 5 4 2      S         ♣ A 6 3
              ♠ A 8 7 6 5 4
              ♡ A J 10
              ◇ Q 3
              ♣ 10 7
```

South is in four spades, and West leads the four of clubs. It is good play to put in the jack from dummy, so that when East wins with the ace, it will not be clear to West that South holds the ten. East returns a heart, the finesse loses, and West plays another heart.

Prospects are poor now, for declarer has lost two tricks and seems sure to lose the ace of diamonds and a trump trick. However, he can give himself a chance by following a subtle sequence of play. Winning with the ace of hearts, he leads the three of diamonds. West, not knowing that his side has a sure trump trick, may think that the contract is going to depend on a diamond guess. The better the player, one might almost say, the more likely he is to play a low diamond. South wins the trick, returns to the ace of spades, runs the ten of clubs, and crosses to the queen of hearts for a discard on the king of clubs.

Note three important elements in this deception by South:

1) He plays the jack of clubs from dummy at trick one. Had he retained K J on the table, the danger of a club finesse and discard would have been more obvious to the opponents.

2) He was careful to win the second heart with the ace so that there would be an entry to dummy later with the queen.

3) He led the low diamond before the ace of spades. Had West seen his partner's king of spades, he would have known that only one diamond trick was needed to defeat the contract.

Example 12

The technique described in the last example is equally valuable at no trumps. Early in the play the declarer leads a suit where he hopes to snatch a trick before turning to his real suit. These tactics may not be at all clear to the defenders.

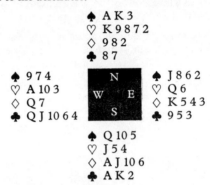

```
              ♠ A K 3
              ♡ K 9 8 7 2
              ◇ 9 8 2
              ♣ 8 7
  ♠ 9 7 4                   ♠ J 8 6 2
  ♡ A 10 3          N       ♡ Q 6
  ◇ Q 7         W       E   ◇ K 5 4 3
  ♣ Q J 10 6 4      S       ♣ 9 5 3
              ♠ Q 10 5
              ♡ J 5 4
              ◇ A J 10 6
              ♣ A K 2
```

After an opening bid of one diamond and a response of one heart, South eventually plays in three no trumps.

West leads the queen of clubs and continues with the jack when South ducks the first trick. South may reasonably expect to make three tricks in diamonds, but three spades, three diamonds, and two clubs leaves him one trick short of his contract.

The simple line is to cross to dummy with a spade and lead a low diamond to the jack. (This is good play, keeping the 9 8 in dummy.) West wins with the queen and plays a third round of clubs, clearing the suit. Declarer crosses to the ace of spades and can pick up three tricks in diamonds, but as soon as he leads a heart, West will go up with the ace and cash two clubs to defeat the contract.

A small difference in timing wins the contract against any defence, as the cards lie. South should lead a heart at trick three. Now what is West to do? If he ducks, the king wins, and South plays on diamonds, as before. And if West goes up with the ace of hearts, then the king of hearts will drop the queen on the next round, and South will have ten tricks on top.

That the queen of hearts should be doubleton was just a lucky accident. Suppose, instead, that East's hearts had been Q J or Q x x. Would West play the ace of hearts on the first round? He would be afraid lest South hold Q x x, in which case the play of the ace would be fatal. By playing on hearts at once South makes the defence quite difficult.

Example 13

One of the most effective ways of slipping through a vital trick is to create the impression that you are on the point of taking a losing finesse. In a suit contract, for example, you have this combination:

J 10 x

Q x x x x   A x x x

K

Quite early in the play you lead the jack from dummy, and East may duck, thinking that you plan to finesse against the queen. (We are assuming here that your object is to make a trick with the king, not to develop a slow trick on the third round of the suit.) With J x x in dummy opposite a singleton king, you may try the same manoeuvre.

At no trumps there are innumerable opportunities to create this kind of illusion. South plays the next hand in three no trumps against a club lead.

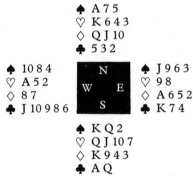

♠ A 7 5
♡ K 6 4 3
♢ Q J 10
♣ 5 3 2

♠ 10 8 4		♠ J 9 6 3
♡ A 5 2	N	♡ 9 8
♢ 8 7	W E	♢ A 6 5 2
♣ J 10 9 8 6	S	♣ K 7 4

♠ K Q 2
♡ Q J 10 7
♢ K 9 4 3
♣ A Q

The jack of clubs runs to the king and ace. By playing on either hearts or diamonds South can establish eight tricks, but no more. He needs, therefore, to slip through one trick in one suit or the other—preferably before the defenders are aware of the danger.

Which suit should he play first, and why? The answer depends on the nature of the holdings visible in dummy. If a diamond is played, the defenders will have no reason to hold up the ace, wherever it lies. Clubs will be cleared, and the enemy will then wait with the ace of hearts and enough clubs to beat the contract.

Declarer's best chance is to lead a heart. Most declarers who had arrived at this conclusion would choose the jack, as though proposing to finesse against the queen. The ten is a slightly more subtle card, however, because this might be from Q 10 9 or from J 10 x. The odds are that West will play low on the ten of hearts, and then, of course, South will switch to diamonds.

We say that West would probably play low, meaning that most defenders would fall for the trap. It is interesting to consider whether West *ought* to play low.

One important inference is available to him. He knows from the play to the first trick that South holds the ace and queen of clubs (since East, with K Q, would play the queen, not the king). There are strong grounds for supposing, also, that South has A Q alone, since with A Q x it would normally be correct to hold up for one round, in the hope of exhausting East.

Now, if his partner had only two clubs, it would be essential for West to retain his only card of entry, the ace of hearts. But if partner has three clubs, West can afford to part with the ace of hearts, trusting that this will not establish nine tricks for the declarer. A top-class player might, therefore, take the ace of hearts and clear the clubs.

Example 14

An experienced player has a host of little tricks at his disposal which he will put into effect almost without needing to think. The fact that most of them will depend for success on imperfect defence does not affect their value. It is, after all, the essence of a trap that it can be avoided.

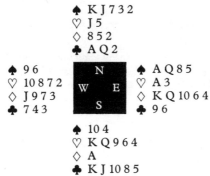

North-South staggered into four hearts by this unconvincing route:

SOUTH	WEST	NORTH	EAST
—	—	—	1 ◇
1 ♡	pass	1 ♠	pass
2 ♣	pass	3 ♣	pass
3 ♡	pass	4 ♡	pass
pass	pass		

There were some grounds for a spade lead, but West led his partner's suit, and the queen was headed by the ace.

It looks as though South will need reasonable luck in the spades and hearts combined. If East holds A Q of spades over the K J, then South cannot afford to lose more than one trump trick.

Most players would think that the contract depended simply on the lie of the cards and would begin with a heart to the jack and ace. Thereafter, they would surely lose two spades and a second trick in trumps to go one down.

South, who was a skilful player, recognized the trump holding as one where, in certain circumstances, the opponents might be trapped into error. He led a club to dummy at trick two and advanced the jack of hearts from the table.

29

It looked to East as though South had entered dummy to lead a heart towards the K 10 or K 10 9. East was not hopeful of a diamond trick, but he had visions of a two-trick defeat by way of this sequence: heart finesse losing to the queen, a spade to the queen, ace of spades and a third spade, which South would ruff; when in with the ace of hearts, he would play a fourth spade, and this might promote a further trump trick.

East played low on the jack of hearts, therefore, and on the next round his ace beat the air.

South, of course, had no means of knowing the exact heart position; but he had seen this combination many times before and knew that the lead of the jack, when East was sure to hold the ace, was capable of gaining a trick.

Example 15

As a defender, what do you do when the queen is presented by
declarer and the cards you can see are:

A 5

K 7 6　　　　　　—

Q led

You will be afraid that South has some holding such as Q J 10 8 or
Q J 9 8, and will hesitate to cover. A clever declarer will sometimes
exploit that uncertainty.

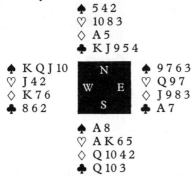

```
               ♠ 5 4 2
               ♡ 10 8 3
               ◇ A 5
               ♣ K J 9 5 4
♠ K Q J 10        N        ♠ 9 7 6 3
♡ J 4 2                    ♡ Q 9 7
◇ K 7 6      W       E     ◇ J 9 8 3
♣ 8 6 2           S        ♣ A 7
               ♠ A 8
               ♡ A K 6 5
               ◇ Q 10 4 2
               ♣ Q 10 3
```

South opens one heart, North bids two clubs, and South rebids two
no trumps; North, somewhat doubtfully, raises to three no trumps.

West leads the king of spades, and South wins the second trick. He
can establish eight tricks by playing on clubs, but even if the spades
are 4-4, there is not much prospect of a ninth trick.

Probably the best chance for the contract is to advance the queen of
diamonds at trick three, before revealing the club support. West will
certainly not expect the queen of diamonds to be an unsupported
honour, and there is a good chance that he will play low, for in many
situations the king could be a costly mistake.

It is on record, incidentally, that a vulnerable grand slam has been
made by way of this lead of an unsupported queen at trick two.

Example 16

Sometimes, with a holding such as Q J 10 x x opposite the ace, declarer wants to induce a cover; at other times, for reasons of entry, he wants to prevent a cover. There is quite an art in choosing the right card to lead.

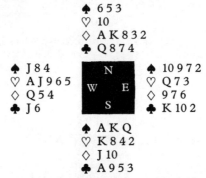

```
              ♠ 6 5 3
              ♡ 10
              ◇ A K 8 3 2
              ♣ Q 8 7 4
  ♠ J 8 4          N          ♠ 10 9 7 2
  ♡ A J 9 6 5   W     E       ♡ Q 7 3
  ◇ Q 5 4          S          ◇ 9 7 6
  ♣ J 6                       ♣ K 10 2
              ♠ A K Q
              ♡ K 8 4 2
              ◇ J 10
              ♣ A 9 5 3
```

South opens a strong no trump, and North raises to three no trumps, expecting his diamond suit to pull plenty of weight.

West leads the six of hearts, East plays the queen, and South is obliged to part with the king. Despite the combined 25 points and the five-card suit in dummy, the situation is not at all favourable. Even if the queen of diamonds is right for him, and even if the suit breaks 3-3, he cannot rely on making five diamond tricks, because of the lack of a quick entry to dummy.

As can be seen, the diamond situation could not be more favourable, but if South leads the jack, West will surely cover, and declarer will be in an unfortunate dilemma: if he ducks the diamond, he must expect the defenders to be in a position to cash four heart winners, and if he covers the queen with the king, he will be limited to two tricks in diamonds (unless the nine is doubleton, and even that will not help much).

South does best, here, to lead the ten, not the jack. This presents West with a really awkward guess. If South has J 10 alone, it is essential to cover, but South may hold something like 10 9 x or 10 x x. In that case, to cover will present declarer with five tricks in diamonds.

When touching honours are held, the best way to slip through the first trick is to lead the lower card. A holding of J 10 opposite A Q x x x is similar to the combination above, and here is another common example:

$$AKJ5$$
$$Q742 \qquad\qquad 863$$
$$10\ 9$$

South has no side entry to the table and needs four tricks. If the ten is led, West knows that he must cover; the nine may be allowed to slip through.

Example 17

When you are seeking to obtain quick discards on a long suit and are hoping to escape a ruff by an opponent, there is an art in concealing your strength. Obviously, if the defender is uncertain whether the card you are leading is a winner or a loser, he will be less inclined to ruff.

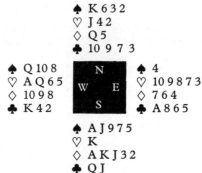

```
              ♠ K 6 3 2
              ♡ J 4 2
              ◇ Q 5
              ♣ 10 9 7 3
  ♠ Q 10 8                    ♠ 4
  ♡ A Q 6 5      N            ♡ 10 9 8 7 3
  ◇ 10 9 8    W     E         ◇ 7 6 4
  ♣ K 4 2        S            ♣ A 8 6 5
              ♠ A J 9 7 5
              ♡ K
              ◇ A K J 3 2
              ♣ Q J
```

South opens one spade, and North raises to two spades. There is no point in showing the diamond suit, so South goes straight to four spades.

West leads the ten of diamonds, and dummy's queen wins. South plays king and another spade, East discarding a heart. It looks now as though one trump, one heart, and two clubs must be lost unless West is obliged to follow to four rounds of diamonds. If that's the situation, declarer will be able to dispose of three clubs from dummy before West is able to ruff.

If South plays off ace, king, and jack of diamonds, West will ruff and cash three winners in hearts and clubs. More subtle play may present West with a problem. South should play off ace and king of diamonds, discarding a club, and then the two. If West is deceived into thinking that his partner has the jack, he may not ruff; then a second club will go away on this trick, and a third club on the next diamond when West, too late, goes in with the queen of spades.

Example 18

The stratagem described in the last example has many subtle variations. Here, the declarer seeks to create the impression that he plans a ruffing finesse.

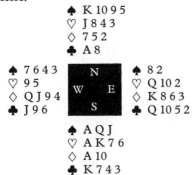

```
              ♠ K 10 9 5
              ♡ J 8 4 3
              ◇ 7 5 2
              ♣ A 8
♠ 7 6 4 3      N        ♠ 8 2
♡ 9 5      W       E    ♡ Q 10 2
◇ Q J 9 4              ◇ K 8 6 3
♣ J 9 6        S        ♣ Q 10 5 2
              ♠ A Q J
              ♡ A K 7 6
              ◇ A 10
              ♣ K 7 4 3
```

South opens two no trumps on his 21 points, and North responds three clubs—Baron convention, asking for four-card suits. The bidding continues:

SOUTH	WEST	NORTH	EAST
2 NT	pass	3 ♣	pass
3 ♡	pass	3 ♠	pass
3 NT	pass	4 ♡	pass
5 ♡	pass	6 ♡	pass
pass	pass		

West opens the queen of diamonds, and South wins with the ace. He cashes the ace and king of hearts, failing to drop the queen. The contract then depends on his being able to discard his losing diamond on the fourth round of spades before the defender, who holds the queen of hearts, has been able to ruff.

If spades are 3-3, there is no problem, and if West has a doubleton, there is no hope. But if East has a doubleton and the outstanding trump, South can lay a trap.

The best sequence is ace of spades, jack of spades overtaken by the king, and ten of spades from dummy. East may form the opinion that South began with A J alone. If East fails to ruff, South wins with the queen, enters dummy with a club, and discards his diamond loser on the fourth spade. East may ruff now, but it is too late.

Example 19

One of the prettiest forms of deception is the 'misleading discard'. In general, when the defenders observe that declarer is taking discards in a particular suit, they conclude that this suit is his weakness and they will attack it as soon as they come in. Exploiting this tendency, the declarer may sometimes discard from a suit where he is well armoured.

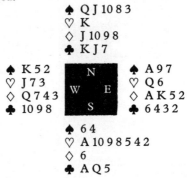

```
              ♠ Q J 10 8 3
              ♡ K
              ◇ J 10 9 8
              ♣ K J 7
  ♠ K 5 2                    ♠ A 9 7
  ♡ J 7 3          N         ♡ Q 6
  ◇ Q 7 4 3     W     E      ◇ A K 5 2
  ♣ 10 9 8          S        ♣ 6 4 3 2
              ♠ 6 4
              ♡ A 10 9 8 5 4 2
              ◇ 6
              ♣ A Q 5
```

The bidding goes:

SOUTH	WEST	NORTH	EAST
—	—	—	1 ◇
2 ♡	pass	2 ♠	pass
3 ♡	pass	4 ♡	pass
pass	pass		

West leads a low diamond to the king and East, thinking that it can hardly matter if the ace is ruffed, leads the ace at trick two. South ruffs and plays a heart to the king. When no honour appears, it is clear that he must lose a trump trick and, presumably, two spades. The position is:

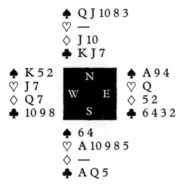

The best chance may seem to be to lead a diamond from dummy and discard a spade. If South does this, West will surely attack spades when in with the queen of diamonds.

Risking two down, South instead leads the ten of diamonds and discards the five of clubs from hand! There is a fair chance now that West will switch to the ten of clubs. Then South will take the ace of clubs, ace of hearts, and discard one spade on the third round of clubs and one on the jack of diamonds.

Example 20

Here is another example of the same kind of play—the misleading discard:

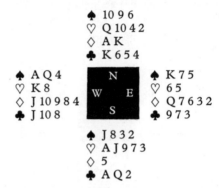

```
              ♠ 10 9 6
              ♡ Q 10 4 2
              ◊ A K
              ♣ K 6 5 4
♠ A Q 4                          ♠ K 7 5
♡ K 8          N                 ♡ 6 5
◊ J 10 9 8 4   W     E           ◊ Q 7 6 3 2
♣ J 10 8          S              ♣ 9 7 3
              ♠ J 8 3 2
              ♡ A J 9 7 3
              ◊ 5
              ♣ A Q 2
```

South plays in four hearts, and West leads the jack of diamonds. The contract will present no difficulty if the heart finesse is right, but if the king is on the wrong side, declarer may lose a heart and three spades. It is true that, given time, South may be able to discard one spade on the king of diamonds and one on dummy's fourth club; but when West comes in with the king of hearts, it is quite likely that he will switch to spades.

To confuse the defence South discards a club, and not a spade, on the second diamond. When the heart finesse loses, West may well switch to the jack of clubs. Declarer then draws trumps, cashes another club, and enters dummy with the queen of hearts. When the clubs break 3-3, he is able to discard two spades and make his contract for the loss of two spades and one heart.

Example 21

When the opponents lead a suit in which the declarer has at least a double guard, it is often a good plan to win the first trick with a higher card than is necessary. By so doing he may avert an attack on a much weaker part of the line.

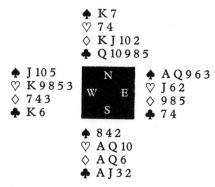

```
              ♠ K 7
              ♡ 7 4
              ◇ K J 10 2
              ♣ Q 10 9 8 5
♠ J 10 5           N          ♠ A Q 9 6 3
♡ K 9 8 5 3    W     E        ♡ J 6 2
◇ 7 4 3            S          ◇ 9 8 5
♣ K 6                        ♣ 7 4
              ♠ 8 4 2
              ♡ A Q 10
              ◇ A Q 6
              ♣ A J 3 2
```

South plays in three no trumps, and West, having no reason to lead a spade, begins with the five of hearts. Suppose, first, that South heads the jack with the queen, enters dummy with a diamond, and takes the club finesse. It will be very obvious to West, when he takes the king of clubs, that there is no future in hearts. His partner's play of the jack of hearts denies the ten, so he can place declarer with A 10. In the circumstances a switch to the jack of spades will be inevitable.

Declarer should foresee this and should win the first trick with the ace of hearts, not the queen. Now, when West comes in with the king of clubs, he may place partner with the queen of hearts and lead a low heart, expecting to run four tricks in the suit.

The point may have occurred to you, 'Shouldn't West be suspicious of this play of the ace on a first round? Isn't it normal for a declarer, with A 10 or A 10 x of the suit led, to hold up the ace for as long as possible?'

In many cases that is a sound argument, but there is a special consideration here. As the critical finesse (in clubs) is to be taken towards West, there can be no point in holding up the ace of hearts to exhaust East. South's immediate play of the ace is not, therefore, a give-away.

Perhaps the best time for this type of stratagem is when the declarer has a double or triple guard, as in these examples:

7 3

Q 9 6 4 2   10 8 5

A K J

West leads the four against a no trump contract, and East plays the ten. If South has reason to fear attack in another suit, he can win with the king instead of the jack.

7 3

A Q 9 5 2   10 4

K J 8 6

West leads the five, and East plays the ten. Again, the way to persuade West to continue this suit when next in the lead is to win the first trick with the king.

Example 22

Declarer's play on the following deal has the same strategical object as in the examples we have just been looking at. Not only does he mislead the defenders into attacking a strongly held position, but at the same time he induces them to present dummy with an entry card.

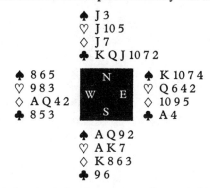

```
              ♠ J 3
              ♡ J 10 5
              ◇ J 7
              ♣ K Q J 10 7 2
♠ 8 6 5                        ♠ K 10 7 4
♡ 9 8 3          N            ♡ Q 6 4 2
◇ A Q 4 2    W     E          ◇ 10 9 5
♣ 8 5 3          S            ♣ A 4
              ♠ A Q 9 2
              ♡ A K 7
              ◇ K 8 6 3
              ♣ 9 6
```

Playing 'five-card majors', South opens one diamond. North responds two clubs, and South now introduces his spades. North can only repeat his clubs, and South transfers to three no trumps.

The other suits having been bid, West leads the nine of hearts. The jack is played from dummy, but East, recognizing the lead as 'top of nothing', does not contribute the queen: he drops the six to show four cards. Recognizing that his best chance of gaining entry to dummy is to persuade the defenders to lead hearts again, South plays the king on his own jack and sets out to develop the clubs.

What is East to think when he comes in with the ace of clubs on the second round of the suit? South has bid diamonds and may hold A Q of spades. On the other hand, it looks as though his hearts are A K alone. East exits with a low heart, therefore; South lets it run to the ten, makes four more tricks in clubs, and can afford to take the spade finesse for an overtrick.

Example 23

Many deceptive plays are no more—and no less—than examples of good timing. South may appear to do nothing special on the deal below, but by doing it at the right moment he traps the defence into an error.

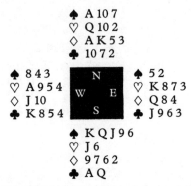

```
              ♠ A 10 7
              ♡ Q 10 2
              ◇ A K 5 3
              ♣ 10 7 2
  ♠ 8 4 3                    ♠ 5 2
  ♡ A 9 5 4      N           ♡ K 8 7 3
  ◇ J 10      W     E        ◇ Q 8 4
  ♣ K 8 5 4      S           ♣ J 9 6 3
              ♠ K Q J 9 6
              ♡ J 6
              ◇ 9 7 6 2
              ♣ A Q
```

North opens a weak no trump, South bids three spades, and North raises to four spades. West leads the jack of diamonds, and declarer wins with dummy's king.

The hands do not fit too well, and South can see four possible losers— two hearts, a diamond and a club. Suppose he draws trumps, then leads a heart, hoping to establish a discard. East will win and attack clubs. The queen is headed by the king, and South must still lose a heart and a diamond.

By playing his cards in the right order South can put East to a severe test. At trick two he should lead the two of hearts from dummy. Clearly, the defence is lost unless East goes up with the king, because South will establish a heart trick before being forced to the club finesse.

Would East go up with the king of hearts at trick two? The great majority of players, certainly, would be caught napping. From East's point of view South might be crossing to a singleton ace of hearts to play spades from hand. To go up with the king of hearts and lead a club might easily be wrong.

Example 24

Good timing, as we have already noted, is often essential when declarer plans an elimination play. So far as possible the early play must not reveal his intentions.

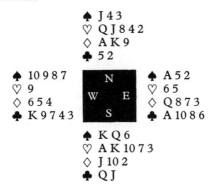

♠ J 4 3
♡ Q J 8 4 2
◇ A K 9
♣ 5 2

♠ 10 9 8 7   ♠ A 5 2
♡ 9   ♡ 6 5
◇ 6 5 4   ◇ Q 8 7 3
♣ K 9 7 4 3   ♣ A 10 8 6

♠ K Q 6
♡ A K 10 7 3
◇ J 10 2
♣ Q J

South is in four hearts, and West leads the ten of spades. East wins with the ace and returns a spade, which South takes with the king.

The best play now is to take just one round of trumps and lead a club from the table. If East plays low, South puts in the jack. West will win and will probably switch to a diamond.

Now the hand is over—for the defence. South goes up with the ace of diamonds, draws the outstanding trump, and cashes the queen of spades, arriving at this position:

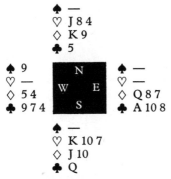

♠ —
♡ J 8 4
◇ K 9
♣ 5

♠ 9   ♠ —
♡ —   ♡ —
◇ 5 4   ◇ Q 8 7
♣ 9 7 4   ♣ A 10 8

♠ —
♡ K 10 7
◇ J 10
♣ Q

South exits with the queen of clubs, and East faces the classical dilemma of returning a diamond into the tenace or conceding a ruff-and-discard.

Both defenders have made a slight error, as it turns out. East would have done better to go up with the ace of clubs on the first round, but this might have resolved a guess for a declarer holding K J instead of Q J; and West, when he won with the king of clubs, could have averted the throw-in by returning a club while his partner still had a card of exit (a trump or a spade).

It must be admitted that South's order of play made the defence difficult. Part of the plan was to take just one round of trumps before touching clubs, because a second round would have given West a chance to signal with a high club.

Suppose that declarer had played in more open fashion, drawing trumps, cashing the third spade, and then exiting with a club. It would have been much easier now for East to take the ace of clubs and exit with a club.

Example 25

One of the most engaging swindles available to the declarer consists of persuading an opponent to surrender a trump trick in a useless cause.

As a rule, when the declarer attempts to cash a winner in a side suit before drawing trumps, his object is to discard a loser, and if the defenders, by ruffing with a low trump, can thwart this project, they are happy to do so. But sometimes the declarer is not trying for a discard at all: he is tempting the defenders to weaken their trump holding.

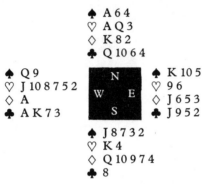

```
              ♠ A 6 4
              ♡ A Q 3
              ◇ K 8 2
              ♣ Q 10 6 4
  ♠ Q 9                      ♠ K 10 5
  ♡ J 10 8 7 5 2            ♡ 9 6
  ◇ A                        ◇ J 6 5 3
  ♣ A K 7 3                  ♣ J 9 5 2
              ♠ J 8 7 3 2
              ♡ K 4
              ◇ Q 10 9 7 4
              ♣ 8
```

The bidding goes:

SOUTH	WEST	NORTH	EAST
pass	1 ♡	dble	pass
2 ♠	pass	2 NT	pass
3 ◇	pass	3 ♠	pass
4 ♠	pass	pass	pass

West leads the king of clubs and switches to the jack of hearts. South (who perhaps ought to have passed three spades) sees that in all probability he is scheduled to lose two trumps and at least one diamond, in addition to the club already surrendered. Nevertheless, he sees a chance and he takes it.

After winning the heart lead with the king, he plays a heart to the ace and follows with the queen from dummy. East, almost certainly, will think that South is playing for a club discard and will insert the five of spades. South overruffs, plays ace and another spade, and later picks up the diamonds for the loss of one trick.

This is one of the most difficult traps to avoid, because with a slightly different hand (better spades, four diamonds and two clubs) declarer would play in just the same way, and it would be essential for East to ruff the third heart.

Example 26

The next deal illustrates two useful principles:

When you can see that a finesse must be taken at some point, take it early, at a moment when the defenders may not find the best continuation.

When the opening lead is in a suit that causes you no worry, make a play, if possible, that will conceal your strength.

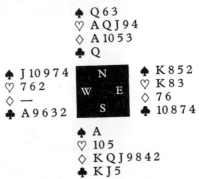

North opens one heart, and South responds two diamonds. When North raises to three diamonds, South wheels out the 'old Black', four no trumps. North bids five hearts to indicate two aces, and South's six diamonds concludes the auction. West leads the jack of spades.

With the heart finesse wrong, it seems unlikely that South will make the slam; nor would he if he won with the ace of spades and played off two rounds of trumps, allowing West to signal in clubs.

But two neat plays put South in with an excellent chance. First, he covers the jack of spades with the queen; when the king is headed by the ace, East is likely to form the opinion that his side has a spade winner.

The next move is to take the heart finesse immediately, before anyone has had a chance to signal. There is a fine chance now that East will attempt to cash the king of spades.

Part II: Deception in defence

Example 27

Most deceptive plays by declarer have their counterpart in defence. Here you will see a reflection of one of the standard moves.

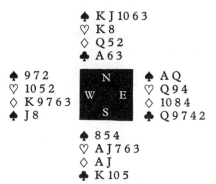

```
              ♠ K J 10 6 3
              ♡ K 8
              ◇ Q 5 2
              ♣ A 6 3
  ♠ 9 7 2          N          ♠ A Q
  ♡ 10 5 2      W     E       ♡ Q 9 4
  ◇ K 9 7 6 3                 ◇ 10 8 4
  ♣ J 8            S          ♣ Q 9 7 4 2
              ♠ 8 5 4
              ♡ A J 7 6 3
              ◇ A J
              ♣ K 10 5
```

The bidding goes:

SOUTH	WEST	NORTH	EAST
1 ♡	pass	1 ♠	pass
1 NT	pass	3 NT	pass
pass	pass		

West leads the six of diamonds, dummy plays low, and the ten is headed by the jack. The natural play at trick two is a spade to dummy's ten.

Suppose, first, that East wins with the queen and clears the diamonds by returning the eight to South's ace. Declarer will realize now that if he plays a second spade he will almost surely lose two spade and three diamond tricks. He is more or less forced to turn to his second string, the heart suit. Here he has better luck. A finesse of the jack, together with the 3-3 break, gives him five heart tricks—enough for game.

East does not know the exact position in hearts, but he can gauge (from the rule of eleven) that South has only one high diamond apart from the jack. In all probability the defence, given time, will make three tricks in diamonds. The way to make sure of this is to win the first spade with the ace, causing declarer to think that the queen lies on the right side for him. After the ace of spades, East clears the diamonds. South repeats the spade finesse, and now East produces the queen, followed by a third diamond.

Example 28

In the next example the defender does not so much lay a trap for the declarer as avoid laying a trap for himself.

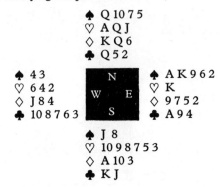

```
                    ♠ Q 10 7 5
                    ♡ A Q J
                    ◇ K Q 6
                    ♣ Q 5 2
  ♠ 4 3                            ♠ A K 9 6 2
  ♡ 6 4 2          N               ♡ K
  ◇ J 8 4      W        E          ◇ 9 7 5 2
  ♣ 10 8 7 6 3      S              ♣ A 9 4
                    ♠ J 8
                    ♡ 10 9 8 7 5 3
                    ◇ A 10 3
                    ♣ K J
```

North opens a strong no trump, and South goes straight to four hearts. West leads the four of spades.

How should East play to the first and second trick? It is fairly certain that if he plays an unsubtle game he will not beat the contract. Thus, suppose he begins with king of spades, ace of spades, ace of clubs and a third spade. South will ruff with the ten of hearts, and West will be unable to overruff. It will not take an Einstein now to realize that the king of hearts is offside. Declarer will go up with the ace on the first round, dropping the singleton king.

Nor will it help, against an intelligent declarer, to win the first two tricks with the king and ace of spades and then, so as not to expose the trump situation, switch to ace and another club. To arrive at the correct inference now involves a slightly longer journey than before, but it should occur to South to wonder why he didn't play a third spade.

East must mask his hand from the beginning. It is best to win the first spade with the ace, then exit with a low club. With nothing to guide him South will take the heart finesse, and East will make the king of hearts, the ace of clubs, and the king of spades.

Example 29

There are several ways of stealing a trump trick in defence. We present three of them in quick succession. The first is achieved by a deceptive peter, which threatens a ruff and causes the declarer to expend a valuable trump.

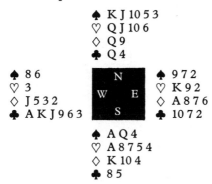

♠ K J 10 5 3
♡ Q J 10 6
◇ Q 9
♣ Q 4

♠ 8 6
♡ 3
◇ J 5 3 2
♣ A K J 9 6 3

♠ 9 7 2
♡ K 9 2
◇ A 8 7 6
♣ 10 7 2

♠ A Q 4
♡ A 8 7 5 4
◇ K 10 4
♣ 8 5

South opens one heart, West overcalls with two clubs, and North bids three hearts. Although he has not much in reserve, South goes to four hearts.

West begins with the king and ace of clubs, and to beat the contract East must be quick-witted. Declarer must surely hold the king of diamonds, so the defence will need to make a trump trick in addition to two clubs and a diamond. This can be achieved only if declarer can be persuaded to ruff the third club with a high trump.

East, therefore, plays a deceptive peter on the first two rounds of clubs, dropping the ten and two, in that order. West (who does not need to be in the plot) will follow with the jack of clubs.

What will South do now? He will have noted East's peter in clubs and will be expecting East to be able to overruff the dummy. He certainly does not want East, with K 9 alone or 9 x x, to be able to insert the nine and force the ace; in all probability he will ruff with the queen. Now East, with K 9 x of hearts over dummy's Q J x, has a sure trump trick.

Example 30

When there is dangerous distribution in the air, the defenders will know about it first and they must be careful not to give the declarer any warning. A spectacular false-card contributes to that end on the following deal.

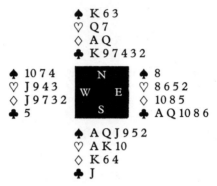

```
                    ♠ K 6 3
                    ♡ Q 7
                    ◇ A Q
                    ♣ K 9 7 4 3 2

        ♠ 10 7 4           ♠ 8
        ♡ J 9 4 3          ♡ 8 6 5 2
        ◇ J 9 7 3 2        ◇ 10 8 5
        ♣ 5                ♣ A Q 10 8 6

                    ♠ A Q J 9 5 2
                    ♡ A K 10
                    ◇ K 6 4
                    ♣ J
```

The bidding goes:

SOUTH	WEST	NORTH	EAST
1 ♠	pass	2 ♣	pass
3 ♠	pass	4 ◇	pass
4 ♡	pass	4 NT	pass
5 ♡	pass	6 ♠	end

West leads his singleton five of clubs, dummy plays low, and East wins with the queen. Knowing that his partner can ruff, East returns a low club. South now thinks to himself:

'It is just possible that West underled the ace of clubs through dummy's suit. (I ought to have gone up with the king, I suppose.) But it is just as likely that West's five was a singleton. Unless West began with all four trumps, I can afford to ruff high, and that seems the sensible thing to do.'

So South ruffs with the jack of spades, and when all follow to a round of trumps, declarer can lay down his cards.

'You gave the show away by returning the low club,' remarks West to his partner. 'We have a better chance if you return the ace.'

East keeps quiet, because he knows he has missed the opportunity for a really clever play. Suppose he wins the first club with the *ace* and returns a low one. South will surely assume that West has the queen of clubs, at least, and will ruff low, seeing no reason to ruff with the jack, which could cost a trump trick if West began with 10 8 7 x.

Example 31

It is sometimes a good idea to ruff with an unnecessarily high trump, to give declarer the impression that this is your *only* trump. This may cause him to follow the wrong line in a situation of this kind:

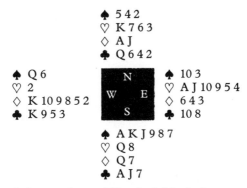

```
              ♠ 5 4 2
              ♡ K 7 6 3
              ◇ A J
              ♣ Q 6 4 2
♠ Q 6              N              ♠ 10 3
♡ 2           W       E          ♡ A J 10 9 5 4
◇ K 10 9 8 5 2       S           ◇ 6 4 3
♣ K 9 5 3                        ♣ 10 8
              ♠ A K J 9 8 7
              ♡ Q 8
              ◇ Q 7
              ♣ A J 7
```

South plays in four spades, and West leads his singleton two of hearts. East plays the ace and returns the nine for West to ruff. As South has bid spades strongly, West's queen of spades is unlikely to have any importance, and even if he has not foreseen the possible consequences, it is good play to ruff with the queen rather than the six.

West then returns the ten of diamonds. What is South to do? It seems foolish to risk the diamond finesse, because if West has no more trumps it is safe to win with the ace of diamonds and discard the queen on dummy's king of hearts. But alas! West produces a low trump after all. South can ruff the next diamond but must lose a club eventually.

There is one rather tricky position where ruffing with an unnecessarily high trump is calculated to induce the declarer to take a losing finesse in the trump suit itself. The trumps are divided as follows:

```
              6 3 2
K 10                     J 4
              A Q 9 8 7 5
```

West has an early opportunity to ruff. He gauges that if he ruffs with the ten declarer will have reason later to drop the king. So he ruffs with the king, and South later takes a deep finesse of the nine, playing East for J 10 x. Well, that is the idea, anyway; it is the sort of play that bridge writers of a certain type attribute to friends whom they wish to flatter.

Example 32

Returning to a more practical world, it is often possible, with a trump holding of Q x x x or Q x x, to cause the declarer to misguess the position of the queen. An opening lead of a low trump from Q x x x is an effective manoeuvre when the suit is distributed like this:

A J 10 5

Q 6 4 2   7

K 9 8 3

West leads the two, and dummy's ten holds the first trick. Declarer will usually play the ace from dummy on the next round, taking the view that West is more likely to have led a singleton than away from the queen.

Here is an amusing little coup worth trying on occasions with Q x x:

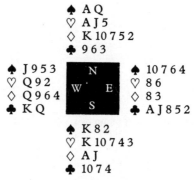

♠ A Q
♡ A J 5
◇ K 10 7 5 2
♣ 9 6 3

♠ J 9 5 3   ♠ 10 7 6 4
♡ Q 9 2   ♡ 8 6
◇ Q 9 6 4   ◇ 8 3
♣ K Q   ♣ A J 8 5 2

♠ K 8 2
♡ K 10 7 4 3
◇ A J
♣ 10 7 4

North opens one diamond, and South responds one heart. North raises to two hearts, and South bids the game.

A club is the most dynamic lead on the West hand, so West begins with the king of clubs. East overtakes the second round with the ace and follows with the jack.

Now West's queen of hearts is more or less dead. Even if South has six hearts to the king, he will be inclined to finesse the right way after East has turned up with five clubs and West with only two.

In the hope of shaking the declarer's confidence, West ruffs the third club with the two of hearts and leads a spade through dummy's A Q. This play is not altogether implausible, for it might be good tactics to force declarer to a decision in spades before he has been able to test the diamonds. As it happens South has no worries in spades but still has to find the queen of trumps. He may change his mind and play East for the queen.

Example 33

Many deceptive plays are possible within a single suit. Most of them depend on an important principle: *play the card you are known to hold or will shortly be known to hold.* These are some examples:

$$A J 4$$
$$Q 10 6 \qquad 8 5 2$$
$$K 9 7 3$$

South leads the three to dummy's jack and follows with the ace. As West is marked with the queen, he must play it now. That leaves declarer with a guess: he may decide, on the next round, to finesse the nine, playing East for 10 8 x x.

$$A Q 7 4 2$$
$$K J 8 3 \qquad 9 5$$
$$10 6$$

This is a side suit in a trump contract. Declarer finesses the queen successfully and follows with the ace. West is known to hold the king and must drop it now; declarer may then hesitate to play another round for fear of being overruffed on his left.

There are many variations of this important position:

$$J 5 2$$
$$10 9 4 \qquad K 6$$
$$A Q 8 7 3$$

Declarer leads low from dummy and finesses the queen. West's nine is going to appear on the next round and he must play it now. By so doing he presents declarer with the option of leading the jack from dummy later, hoping to pin the ten. If West does not play the nine (or ten), declarer will play the ace on the next round, as his only chance for five tricks will be to drop the king. Because the play of the nine is the only way to create a guess, this is known as an 'obligatory false card'.

The deceptive play with the following holding is well known, but the declarer still has to make a decision.

A Q 7 5 2

K 10   8 6 4

J 9 3

South leads the three from hand. West's king is a dead duck, in the sense that it will fall on the next round, so he plays it at once. Declarer wins with the ace and has the option now of finessing the nine on the way back, playing East for 10 x x x. The same play can be made with Q 10 when the hand on the left holds A K x x x and the declarer J 9 x.

In general, a defender must always be alert for opportunities to present the declarer with alternative choices. Thus West must be careful to drop the jack or ten on the first round in this type of position:

5

J 10 7   A 4

K Q 9 8 6 3 2

Declarer leads the five from dummy towards his long suit. East plays low, and the king wins. West must play one of his honour cards so that South will have to guess on the next round whether to lead a low card or the queen.

Example 34

Sometimes a deceptive play will give declarer not just a guess but a definite tilt in the wrong direction. Here, East brings off a pretty coup:

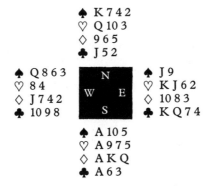

```
                  ♠ K 7 4 2
                  ♡ Q 10 3
                  ◇ 9 6 5
                  ♣ J 5 2
   ♠ Q 8 6 3         N          ♠ J 9
   ♡ 8 4                        ♡ K J 6 2
   ◇ J 7 4 2      W     E       ◇ 10 8 3
   ♣ 10 9 8         S          ♣ K Q 7 4
                  ♠ A 10 5
                  ♡ A 9 7 5
                  ◇ A K Q
                  ♣ A 6 3
```

South opens two no trumps, and North raises to three no trumps. Against this bidding the lead of a low spade or diamond does not hold much appeal, so West begins with the ten of clubs. South holds up for two rounds and wins the third club.

There are only seven tricks on top, and evidently South must play on hearts for the extra tricks he needs. With sufficient entries it is usual to lead the queen first with this type of holding, but there is little to choose between one method and another, and on this occasion, with only entry to the table, it is natural to begin with a low card to the ten.

East should realize that if he wins with the jack his king will inevitably die the death when South crosses to dummy with a spade and leads the queen. Following the general principle of playing the card you will shortly be known to hold, East wins this trick with the king, not the jack. He cashes the thirteenth club and exits with a diamond.

Thinking that the jack of hearts is on his left, South plays a heart to the queen and a heart back to the ace, discovering that East, after all, holds the guarded jack. Now declarer has nowhere to go for his ninth trick; having lost four tricks already, he cannot give up a spade even if West has thrown one.

It is worth noting that this particular deception can be played from the other side of the park, as it were.

A 10 4

K J 6   8 5 2

Q 9 7 3

Declarer leads the ten from dummy and plays low from hand. If West wins with the jack, South will run the nine when next in the lead and will make the rest of the tricks. But if West wins with the king, South will surely play the ace next and then finesse the nine, losing to the jack.

Example 35

A critical position often arises on the second trick in a no trump contract. West leads from his longest suit, East wins and returns the suit, which is divided in this fashion:

$$7\ 4$$
$$A\ 10\ 8\ 6\ 3\ 2 \qquad K\ 5$$
$$Q\ J\ 9$$

West can tell that his partner has no more cards of the suit and we will suppose, further, that West has no chance of regaining the lead. Thus, the suit is virtually dead.

Now West has three possible courses of action. The worst, unless some other line of attack is definitely promising, is to win with the ace and then seek fresh pastures. This tells the declarer (a) that the suit is divided 6-2, as otherwise West would have ducked the second round; and (b) that West has no entry card. This will enable him to place all the important cards and greatly simplify his task.

Secondly, West may duck the return. The best card to play is the three, leaving declarer to suppose that East has the two and that the suit is divided 5-3. This is sound play. One of the advantages is that South, placing West with a five-card suit, may attempt some kind of throw-in and be disappointed to find that West has a longer suit than expected.

Thirdly, West may win with the ace and play a third round, as though he had a likely entry card. This may cause declarer to misplace one of the key cards, but whether it will make any difference to the natural sequence of play will depend on the special circumstances.

It is particularly important for a defender who has only a *potential* card of entry not to make it clear to everyone that he has lost touch with his partner. This hand from a team-of-four match illustrates the point:

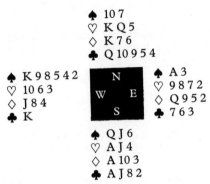

♠ 10 7
♡ K Q 5
◇ K 7 6
♣ Q 10 9 5 4

♠ K 9 8 5 4 2   ♠ A 3
♡ 10 6 3   ♡ 9 8 7 2
◇ J 8 4   ◇ Q 9 5 2
♣ K   ♣ 7 6 3

♠ Q J 6
♡ A J 4
◇ A 10 3
♣ A J 8 2

At both tables South opened one no trump and became the declarer in three no trumps.

West led his fourth best spade, East won with the ace and returned the three. Knowing that his partner held no more spades, West at one table saw no point in ducking: he won with the king and cleared the suit.

Now South had an obvious safety play. Since he could afford to lose the lead to East, but not to West, he laid down the ace of clubs and made the rest of the tricks.

At the other table West ducked the spade return, dropping the four. From South's point of view the spades could well be 5-3. If so, he had to take the best chance in clubs, which, of course, is to finesse for the king. When this lost, he was two down—a difference of four tricks between the two tables.

Example 36

It is good play, when defending against three no trumps, to refrain from cashing the *fourth* defensive trick unless you can see where the fifth is coming from. For one thing, though this is outside the scope of the present book, you make it much easier for declarer to execute a squeeze if you create the situation in which he needs all the remaining tricks. Apart from that, by concealing the fact that you have a winner to play you may induce the declarer to take a finesse towards your hand instead of towards your partner.

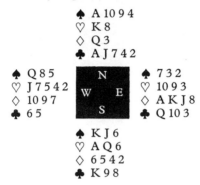

```
                  ♠ A 10 9 4
                  ♡ K 8
                  ◇ Q 3
                  ♣ A J 7 4 2
  ♠ Q 8 5          N          ♠ 7 3 2
  ♡ J 7 5 4 2                 ♡ 10 9 3
  ◇ 10 9 7      W     E       ◇ A K J 8
  ♣ 6 5            S          ♣ Q 10 3
                  ♠ K J 6
                  ♡ A Q 6
                  ◇ 6 5 4 2
                  ♣ K 9 8
```

South plays in three no trumps and West leads the ten of diamonds in preference to a low heart. East makes the first three tricks with high diamonds, dummy discarding the eight of hearts. What next?

Suppose, first, that East cashes his fourth diamond, forcing a club discard from dummy, then exits with a heart. The correct play for declarer now is to cash the ace and king of clubs. If the queen does not appeal, a successful finesse in spades will produce the necessary tricks.

East should appreciate that there is no hurry to cash the fourth diamond. At trick four he switches to the ten of hearts. Now, from the declarer's point of view West is more likely than East to hold the missing eight of diamonds. He may well think that his best line is to take the natural finesse in clubs, expecting to make four clubs, three hearts, and two spades. (It would not be correct now to play ace and king of clubs, then take the spade finesse; this would lose the contract if East held the guarded queen of clubs and the queen of spades.)

Example 37

Many of the best deceptive plays at no trumps are linked to problems of communication. A player who has a long suit that has yet to be established may need to risk a dangerous hold-up so that his entry card will not be lost too soon.

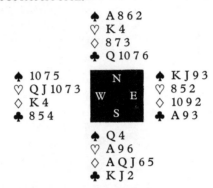

```
              ♠ A 8 6 2
              ♡ K 4
              ◇ 8 7 3
              ♣ Q 10 7 6

    ♠ 10 7 5                    ♠ K J 9 3
    ♡ Q J 10 7 3       N        ♡ 8 5 2
    ◇ K 4          W       E    ◇ 10 9 2
    ♣ 8 5 4            S        ♣ A 9 3

              ♠ Q 4
              ♡ A 9 6
              ◇ A Q J 6 5
              ♣ K J 2
```

South opens one diamond, North responds one spade, and South jumps to two no trumps. North bids three no trumps, and West leads the queen of hearts.

The natural play for declarer is to win the second heart in dummy and lead a diamond to the queen. It looks risky for West to hold up his king, but the odds are that South holds A Q J in diamonds and will repeat the finesse later; meanwhile, if West gives up his only entry card, he has little hope of beating the contract.

West should play low, therefore, on the queen of diamonds. Declarer switches to clubs, playing the king, followed by the jack. East wins the second round and clears the hearts. Declarer has eight tricks in sight now (three clubs, two hearts, ace of spades, queen, and ace of diamonds), and certainly the natural play for a ninth trick is to finesse again in diamonds; West wins and cashes two hearts to defeat the contract.

Example 38

Despite the general injunction that high cards should be used to kill an opponent's high cards, there are many situations where it is fairly safe to hold up high cards and there may be considerable advantage in so doing. Take this familiar position:

K 6 4

J 9   A 8 3

Q 10 7 5 2

South, who has bid the suit, leads low to the king. It is really not necessary for East to part with his ace, unless this quick entry is needed for a special purpose. To hold up the ace is good deception, because declarer will temporarily assume that the ace is on his left. If East needs to protect his own entries, then the hold-up is even more valuable. Declarer, on the next round, will surely finesse the ten and lose to West's jack.

It is especially important not to part with the king in this kind of situation:

A 6 2

10 6   K J 5

Q 9 8 4 3

South initiates the suit by leading the ace from dummy and following with the two. East may play the jack. From declarer's angle this might be from J 10 x; if South takes that view, he will duck, hoping to bring down the king from West.

Players who know this last position often fail to realize that the same stratagem can be followed with A J x, as in this example:

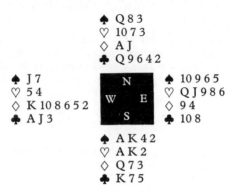

♠ Q 8 3
♡ 10 7 3
◇ A J
♣ Q 9 6 4 2

♠ J 7
♡ 5 4
◇ K 10 8 6 5 2
♣ A J 3

♠ 10 9 6 5
♡ Q J 9 8 6
◇ 9 4
♣ 10 8

♠ A K 4 2
♡ A K 2
◇ Q 7 3
♣ K 7 5

The bidding goes:

SOUTH	WEST	NORTH	EAST
1 ♠	pass	2 ♠	pass
2 NT	pass	3 NT	pass
pass	pass		

West leads the five of diamonds, and the jack is played from dummy. In a situation of this sort, where it is plain that East does not hold a card higher than the jack, the modern style is to show distribution. East drops the nine, therefore, to indicate an even number.

At trick two declarer leads a low club to the king. This is the decisive moment. If West parts with the ace and clears the diamonds, South will test the spades and then play a low club from hand, ducking the trick to East's ten. As East has no more diamonds, declarer will end up with ten tricks.

Knowing that he must preserve his entry card, the ace of clubs, West must duck the first club. When the jack appears on the next round, South will surely play low from dummy, as indeed would be right if West held J 10 x and East A x. The Jack holds, and West clears the diamonds. As before, South will try to find his ninth trick in spades, but when this fails he will play another club, and West will run off enough diamonds to beat the contract.

Example 39

We made the point above that it was not always necessary to use one's own high cards to kill those of an opponent. In much the same way it is *not* as a rule necessary to keep one's honour cards guarded. If you are destined to make a trick with the queen from Q x x, you will probably make it from Q x as well, and if a king sits over an ace or A Q, it will make even if single.

Good players don't like to be end-played; that is to say, they don't like to be thrown in and forced to lead away from a minor tenace (such as from K x into A Q). The best way to avoid this is to unguard kings and queens quite early in the play. This is a common type of hand:

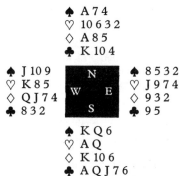

```
              ♠ A 7 4
              ♡ 10 6 3 2
              ◇ A 8 5
              ♣ K 10 4
♠ J 10 9      ┌─────────┐      ♠ 8 5 3 2
♡ K 8 5       │    N    │      ♡ J 9 7 4
◇ Q J 7 4     │ W     E │      ◇ 9 3 2
♣ 8 3 2       │    S    │      ♣ 9 5
              └─────────┘
              ♠ K Q 6
              ♡ A Q
              ◇ K 10 6
              ♣ A Q J 7 6
```

South opens two no trumps, North raises to four no trumps, and South, relying on his five-card suit, accepts the invitation and bids six no trumps. West leads the jack of spades.

South has eleven tricks on top, and it looks at first as though the contract will depend on the heart finesse. However, there may be chances for an end-play, so South, after winning with the king of spades, plays out five rounds of clubs, discarding a heart and a diamond from the table. Most defenders in West's position would discard a diamond and heart. Assuming that East throws a diamond, a spade, and a heart, the position after six tricks will be:

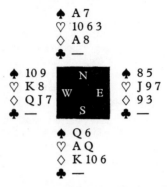

```
                    ♠ A 7
                    ♡ 10 6 3
                    ◇ A 8
                    ♣ —
    ♠ 10 9                        ♠ 8 5
    ♡ K 8          N              ♡ J 9 7
    ◇ Q J 7     W     E           ◇ 9 3
    ♣ —            S              ♣ —
                    ♠ Q 6
                    ♡ A Q
                    ◇ K 10 6
                    ♣ —
```

To improve his count of the hand South will play off two rounds of
spades. When all follow, he will know that no spades are left.
Recalling that each defender has thrown one diamond, he will follow
with ace, king, and another diamond, knowing that this will force the
defenders to open up the hearts. As West wins the third diamond, he
will have to lead a heart from K x at trick twelve.

'Pity,' West will say. 'I had control of both red suits.'

Well, that was obvious from the beginning. As soon as his partner
has shown out on the third round of clubs, West should count the
declarer for five clubs, three spades, two diamonds, and a heart on
top. That is eleven tricks, and West must be very conscious of the
danger of being thrown in. On the two clubs he must discard the five
and eight of hearts. Declarer may now finesse in hearts. If, instead,
he tries the same end-play in diamonds, West must play the four and
jack on the first two rounds. When South follows with a third
diamond, West unexpectedly produces the queen and seven.

On many hands, especially those played in two or three no trumps,
the ending cannot be so easily foreseen. It is still good tactics, both in
a technical and a psychological sense, to confuse the declarer by
unguarding kings and queens.